ODDS 'N' ENDS ART

Gillian Souter

Gareth Stevens Publishing
A WORLD ALMANAC EDUCATION GROUP COMPANY

★ Before You Start ★

Some of these projects can get messy, so make sure your work area is covered with newspaper. For projects that need paint, you can use acrylic paint, poster paint, or any other kind of paint that is labeled nontoxic. Ask an adult to help you find paints that are safe to use. You will also need an adult's help to make some of the projects, especially when you have to stitch fabric, poke holes with pointed objects, use a craft knife or any other sharp cutting utensils, or bake something in an oven.

Please visit our web site at: www.garethstevens.com
For a free color catalog describing Gareth Stevens Publishing's
list of high-quality books and multimedia programs,
call 1-800-542-2595 or fax your request to (414) 332-3567.

Library of Congress Cataloging-in-Publication Data

Souter, Gillian.
    Odds 'n' ends art / by Gillian Souter.
      p. cm. — (Handy crafts)
    Includes bibliographical references and index.
    Summary: Provides instructions for making such items as a clay pen holder, paper rockets, monster masks, sock puppets, and a "weather reporter."
    ISBN 0-8368-3051-2 (lib. bdg.)
    1. Handicraft—Juvenile literature. 2. Refuse and refuse disposal—Juvenile literature. [1. Handicraft.]
I. Title. II. Series.
TT160.S652   2002
745.5—dc21
                                     2001055097

This edition first published in 2002 by
Gareth Stevens Publishing
A World Almanac Education Group Company
330 West Olive Street, Suite 100
Milwaukee, Wisconsin 53212 USA

This U.S. edition © 2002 by Gareth Stevens, Inc. Original edition published as *Fun to Make* in 2001 by Off the Shelf Publishing, 32 Thomas Street, Lewisham NSW 2049, Australia. Projects, text, and layout © 2001 by Off the Shelf Publishing. Additional end matter © 2002 by Gareth Stevens, Inc.

Illustrations: Clare Watson
Photographs: Andre Martin
Cover design: Joel Bucaro and Scott M. Krall
Gareth Stevens editor: JoAnn Early Macken

Printed in the United States of America

1 2 3 4 5 6 7 8 9 06 05 04 03 02

Contents

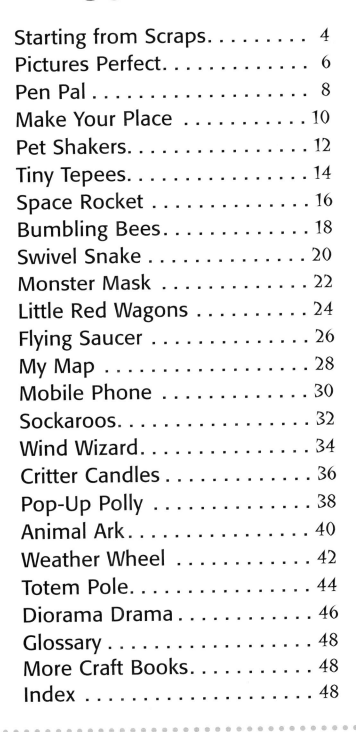

Starting from Scraps

Don't throw out those bits and pieces and unused objects. Save them for your next art or craft project. Keep a craft basket and start collecting interesting items.

Different types of paper and cardboard are basic materials for many craft creations. Save cereal boxes and greeting cards. You can even paint plain paper instead of buying colored paper.

Keep cardboard tubes, of all sizes, from rolls of toilet paper, wrapping paper, paper towels, and plastic wrap. Save empty egg cartons, matchboxes, and plastic bottles. Collect corks, jar lids, and wooden ice cream sticks.

When you lose a sock, don't throw out the other one. Use it to make a sock puppet!

You might have to buy a few of your art and craft materials. You will need pipe cleaners, drinking straws, modeling clay, and paper cups and plates for the projects in this book.

Pictures Perfect

Draw a design, paint a pal or a pet, and present your pictures with pride!

You Will Need
- pencil
- ruler
- white cardboard
- scissors
- paints and markers
- paintbrush
- string or thread
- glue
- ice cream sticks

1 Draw a 4-inch (10-centimeter) square on a piece of white cardboard and cut it out.

2 Draw a picture in the center of the square. Color the picture with paints or markers.

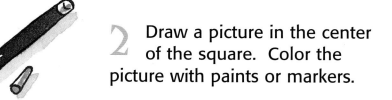

3 Cut a piece of string or thread and glue it onto the back of the cardboard square, at the top, to make a hanging loop.

4 Paint eight ice cream sticks and let them dry. (You can buy ice cream sticks in packets at a craft store.)

5 Glue together two ice cream sticks along the top of your picture and two along the bottom. Then glue two ice cream sticks along each side.

★ **Helpful Hint** ★
If you draw a picture on paper, you can glue it onto cardboard before you make the frame.

Pen Pal

Put a porcupine to work watching your pencils and pens or crayons.

┌─────────────────────┐
You Will Need
- plastic bag
- air-drying clay
- blunt knife
- pens and pencils
- acrylic paint
- paintbrush
- varnish
└─────────────────────┘

1 Cover your work area with a big plastic bag. Roll a large ball of clay for a body and a smaller one for a head. Shape the head with your fingers to make a snout.

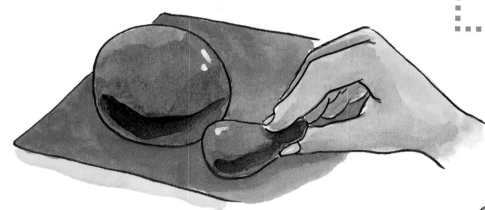

2 Roll four small balls of clay and shape each one into a paw. Use the edge of a blunt knife to mark the toes.

3 Press the head and paws firmly onto the body. Use the end of a pen cap to make eyes on the head.

4 Push a pen or a pencil into the back of the body and twist it gently until it fits loosely. Make more holes the same way, but be careful not to make them too close together.

5 Leave your creature in a warm, dry place until the clay has completely hardened. Paint the animal a bright color, then brush on a coat of varnish.

★ **Helpful Hint** ★
If a piece of your porcupine breaks off while the clay is drying, just glue the piece back on!

Make Your Place

Eat your meals in style on a personal placemat you make yourself. Make a matching set for your whole family!

1 Cut two pieces of fabric that are each 15 inches by 11 inches (38 cm by 28 cm).

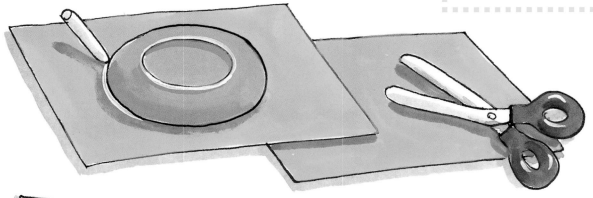

2 Lay a small plate upside down on one piece of fabric and draw around the plate with chalk. Draw a knife and a fork next to the plate.

3 Thread a needle and knot one end of the thread. Sew along the chalk lines with small, even stitches. Hide any knots at the back of the fabric.

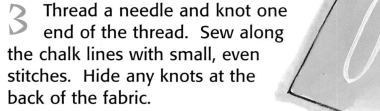

4 Lay the two pieces of fabric together with the stitching on top. Pin bias tape around the edges.

5 Sew through the tape and both layers of fabric with long stitches. You might need a thimble if the sewing gets tough!

★ Helpful Hint ★
Draw the fork on the left side of the plate and the knife on the right side.

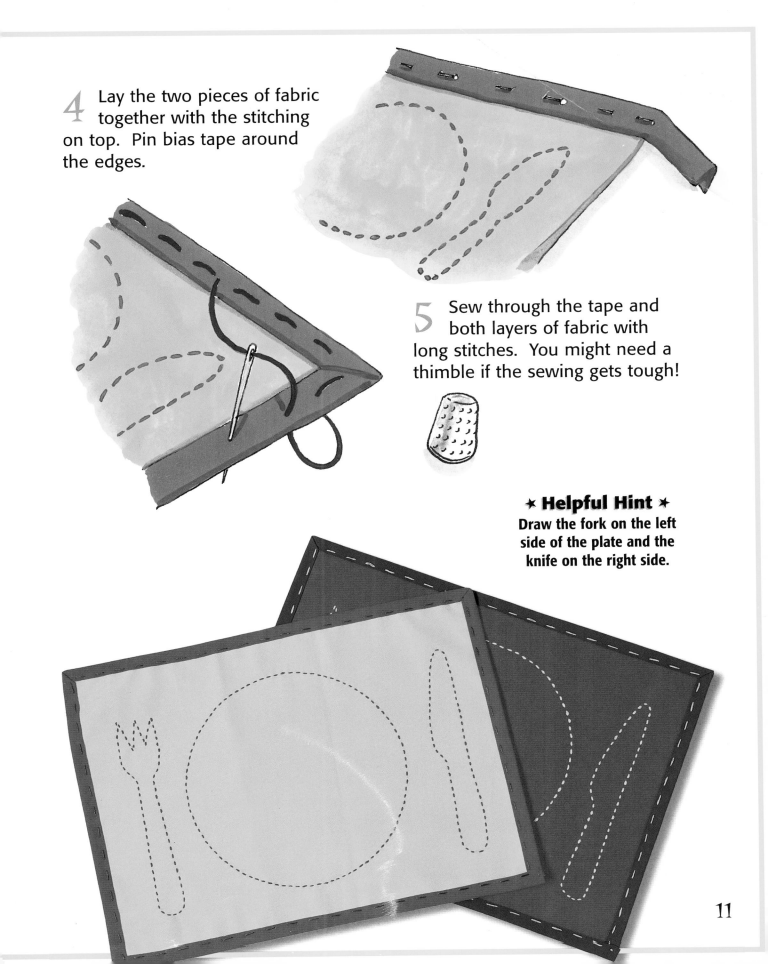

11

Pet Shakers

Rice makes these papier-mâché pets rattle. You make the music!

1 Roll two balls of modeling clay, one larger than the other. Stick them together to make an animal shape.

You Will Need
- modeling clay
- white glue
- water
- bowl
- newspaper
- sharp knife
- dry rice
- masking tape
- paints
- paintbrush
- pencil

2 Mix equal amounts of white glue and water in a bowl. Tear newspaper into narrow strips.

3 Dip each newspaper strip in the glue and water mixture and stick it onto the clay animal shape. Overlap the strips as you work, covering the clay with five layers of newspaper strips. Let the papier-mâché dry completely.

4 Ask an adult to cut the shape in half, lengthwise, with a sharp knife. Carefully pull out the modeling clay.

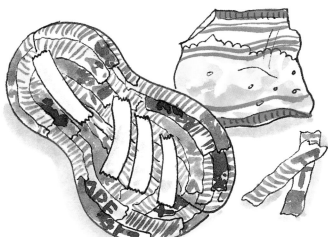

5 Put a spoonful of dry rice in one half of the papier-mâché shape, then tape the halves together with masking tape. Glue newspaper strips over the seam and let the glue dry.

6 Paint the animal shape white. Draw in the animal's features with a pencil, then fill in the details with paints.

★ **Helpful Hint** ★
A coat of clear varnish is a nice finishing touch.

Tiny Tepees

American Indians painted their
homes with beautiful designs.
Make a miniature tepee and
decorate it with your own designs!

You Will Need
- compass
- pencil
- strong paper
- scissors
- crayons or markers
- glue
- wooden skewers

1 Set a compass to 4 inches (10 cm).
Draw a circle on strong paper and
cut it out. Reset the compass to $3/4$ inch
(2 cm). Draw a small circle in the center
of the large circle.

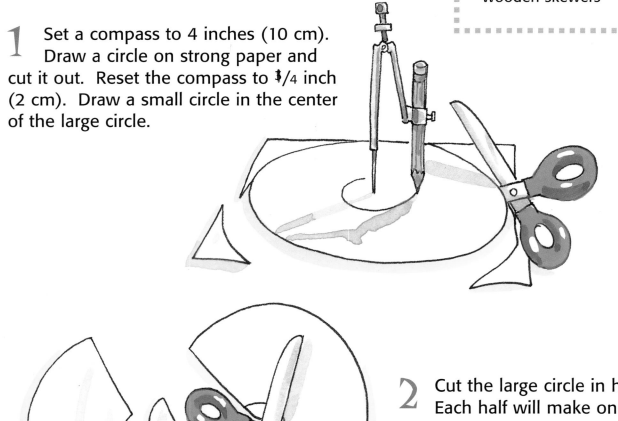

2 Cut the large circle in half.
Each half will make one
tepee. Cut out the small semi-
circles and throw them away.

3 Decorate one side of each large semicircle with crayons or markers.

4 Curl each semicircle into a cone and glue together the overlapping edges.

5 For each tepee, cut wooden skewers into three 4 ½-inch (11-cm) pieces. Glue these pieces inside the tepee so the skewers stick out through the small hole at the top.

★ **Helpful Hint** ★
To make a door for your tepee, cut a small slit into the bottom edge of the cone and fold the paper back.

15

Space Rocket

**Count down to a total blast!
This sparkling spaceship is
out of this world!**

1 Save a cardboard tube from a roll of toilet paper. Cover the tube with aluminum foil, tucking the ends in neatly.

2 Cut long, narrow strips of red and yellow or orange crepe paper. Gather the strips together at one end.

3 Tie a looped piece of string or narrow ribbon around the crepe-paper strips. Thread the string through the tube.

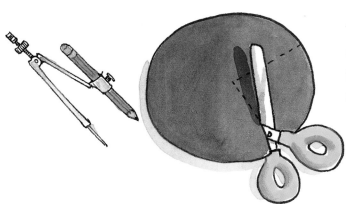

4 Set a compass to 1 ½ inches (4 cm). Draw a circle on thin cardboard and cut it out. Divide the circle into four equal parts. Cut out one of the parts.

5 Curl the rest of the circle around the string to make a cone. Glue down the overlapping edge, then glue the cone onto the tube.

6 Cut out two cardboard triangles. Fold over one side of each triangle to make a flap. Dab glue on the flaps and stick one triangle onto each side of the rocket.

★ Bright Idea ★
For your next party, plan a space theme and decorate the room with rockets!

17

Bumbling Bees

These busy buzzers are so easy to make, you can have a whole swarm of them!

You Will Need

- acrylic paints
- paintbrush
- Styrofoam balls
- scissors
- foil-coated cardboard
- paper clips
- pipe cleaners
- thread or string

1 Paint some Styrofoam balls yellow. After they dry, paint several black rings around each ball. Add two dots of black paint for eyes.

2 Cut pairs of wings out of foil-coated cardboard. Cut two slots in each ball with the blade of a scissors and push a cardboard wing into each slot.

3 Open a paper clip to make a wire loop. Push the two ends of the paper clip into the top of a ball.

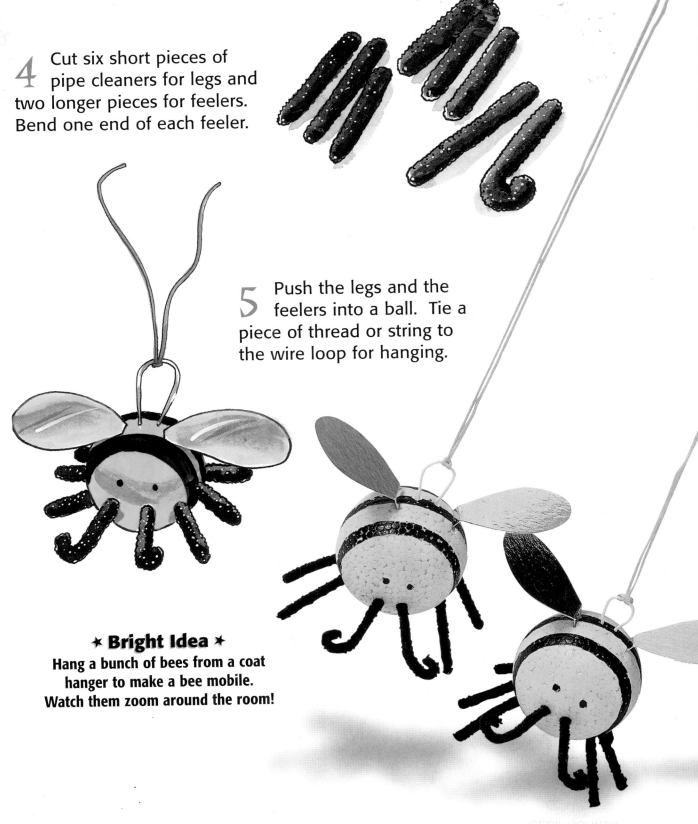

4 Cut six short pieces of pipe cleaners for legs and two longer pieces for feelers. Bend one end of each feeler.

5 Push the legs and the feelers into a ball. Tie a piece of thread or string to the wire loop for hanging.

★ **Bright Idea** ★
Hang a bunch of bees from a coat hanger to make a bee mobile. Watch them zoom around the room!

Swivel Snake

With segments that swivel, this snazzy serpent slithers and slides!

1 Across a sheet of thin cardboard, draw lines 2 ½ inches (6 cm) apart. Using a protractor, draw in another set of lines 2 ½ inches (6 cm) apart but at a 60° angle to the first set of lines. Now you have rows of diamond shapes.

2 Cut along the lines and set aside two diamonds. Decorate the rest of the diamonds with a marker and punch a hole in each side (as shown).

3 Bend each diamond into a ring. Glue together the overlapping points. Each ring is one segment of the snake's body.

4 Hook the body segments together with paper fasteners to form a long chain.

5 Punch one hole in each of the two remaining diamonds. Bend and glue these diamonds into rings, then fasten one to each end of the snake.

6 On one end, draw in two eyes and glue on a forked tongue.

★ **Bright Idea** ★
**Use different colors of paper
to make a snake
with patterned skin!**

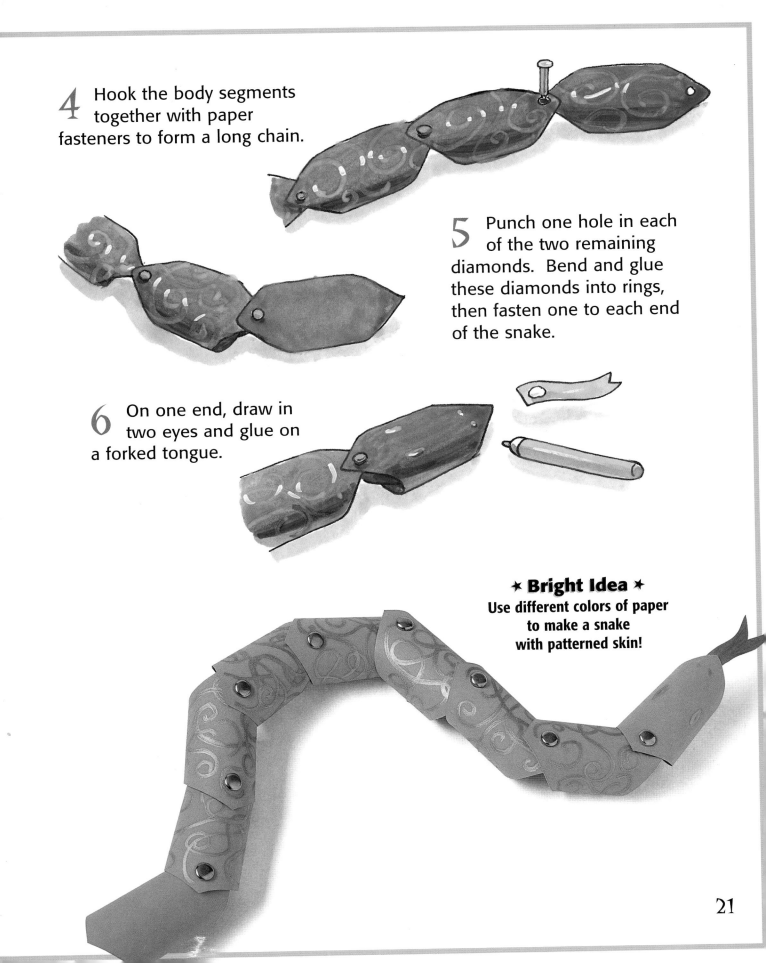

Monster Mask

**Fool your friends with a
frightening face or
a goofy disguise.**

1 Cut the back and the base off of an empty cereal box. Cut open both corners at the top of the box. Bend the top and side flaps so the box is inside out. Then tape the flaps closed.

2 Hold the box against your face to decide where the nose and eye holes should be. Ask a friend to mark them with a pencil, then cut them out.

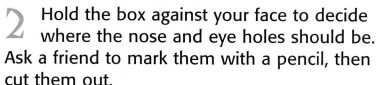

3 Paint the mask and decorate it with yarn, feathers, tissue paper, sequins, or anything else you can find.

4 Cut a silly nose or a big beak out of colored paper. Glue it over the nose hole.

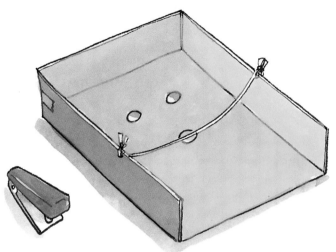

5 Punch a hole in each side flap. Cut a piece of string or elastic thread to fit around your head and tie each end of the string to one side of the mask.

★ Bright Idea ★
Wear your mask to a costume party or for a game of make-believe!

Little Red Wagons

This little train has a string of cars you can fill with tiny trinkets.

1 Paint the covers and trays of five empty matchboxes. Draw around a button or a small coin on cardboard to make twelve circles for wheels. Cut out all of the circles.

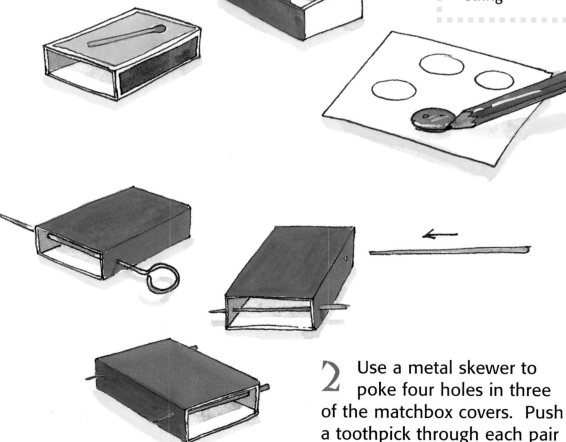

2 Use a metal skewer to poke four holes in three of the matchbox covers. Push a toothpick through each pair of holes.

3 Poke a hole in the center of each wheel. Push a wheel onto the point of each toothpick. If the wheels are loose, glue them in place.

4 Glue two more matchboxes onto a wheeled cover (as shown) to make an engine. Poke a hole near the front of the top matchbox and push in a piece of a drinking straw for a smokestack.

5 Spread glue on the tops of the other wheeled covers. Lay a piece of string over them and stick a tray on top of each cover. Glue one end of the string to the engine.

★ Bright Idea ★
Connect more cars to make a longer train!

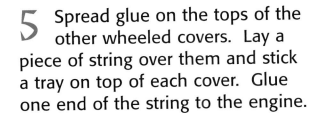

25

Flying Saucer

This awesome alien spaceship is not just any old paper saucer. It really flies!

1 Glue together two paper plates so they are facing each other.

2 Cut off the top of a paper cup to about a third of the way down. Snip evenly spaced cuts around the new rim. Bend the cut sections back to make a lot of small tabs.

3 Put a dab of glue on the inside of each tab. Stick the overturned cup to the center of the plate base.

4 Decorate the flying saucer with markers and stickers. To avoid any crash landings, launch your spaceship in an open area outdoors — and watch it soar!

★ **Helpful Hint** ★

Do not decorate your spaceship with paint, especially if you are using thin paper plates. Paint can make paper plates damp and soft.

My Map

Build a model of your neighborhood, including your house and the scenery around it.

1 Paint a large sheet of cardboard green on one side and let it dry.

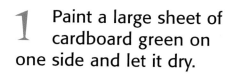

2 Paint a box the same color as your house. If your house has a peaked roof, glue on a piece of folded corrugated cardboard. Glue the house in the middle of the painted cardboard sheet.

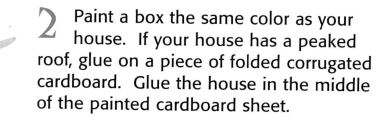

3 On the cardboard sheet, paint the streets around your house.

28

4 To make trees, snip along one edge of a piece of green paper (as shown). Roll up the paper and tape it closed. Bend down the snipped pieces to look like branches. Glue the trees onto your map.

matchbox

dot stickers

pipe cleaners

cork

5 Add other buildings, such as a school, shops, or your friends' houses. You can also add traffic lights or anything else near your house.

★ **Bright Idea** ★
Make street signs to label the streets on your map.

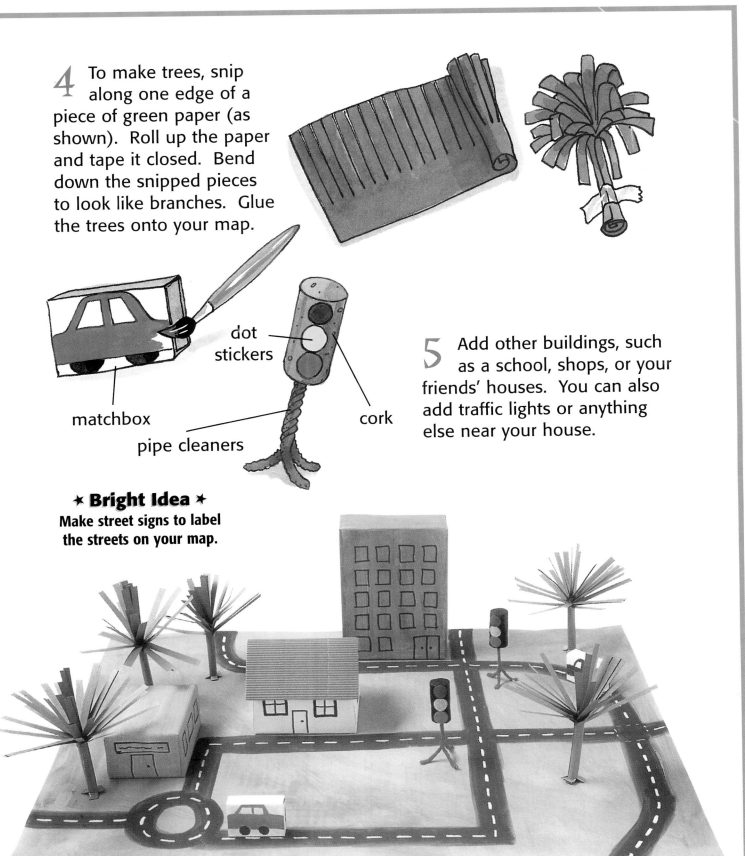

Mobile Phone

**Try this project with a pal
so you can chat together!**

You Will Need
- long box
- scissors
- glue
- aluminum foil
- drinking straw
- markers
- paper
- small button

1 Find or make a suitable box. You can shorten a large toothpaste box by trimming off one end, cutting new flaps, and gluing them down.

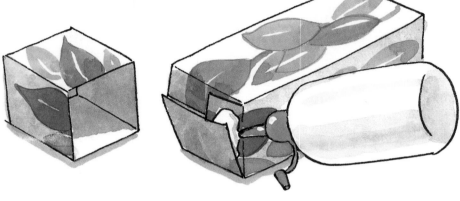

2 Cover the box with aluminum foil, folding the ends in neatly.

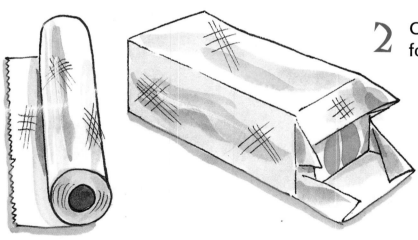

3 Poke a hole in one end of the foil-covered box with the point of a scissors. Push a drinking straw into the hole for the antenna.

4 Draw a black square on paper and color it in with markers. Cut out the square and glue it near the top of the phone.

5 Place a small button on paper. Draw around it and color in the circle. Make at least fourteen of these circles.

6 Draw a number or a symbol in each circle. Cut the circles out and glue them onto the phone.

★ Helpful Hint ★
Use round stickers to make this project even easier!

Sockaroos

These hand puppets are a clever way to use those odd socks you find in the drawer!

You Will Need

• socks
• needle and thread
• buttons
• yarn
• cardboard
• scissors

1 Pull a sock over your hand so the heel is at the back of your hand, near the top of your wrist. Poke in the toe between your thumb and fingertips to make a mouth.

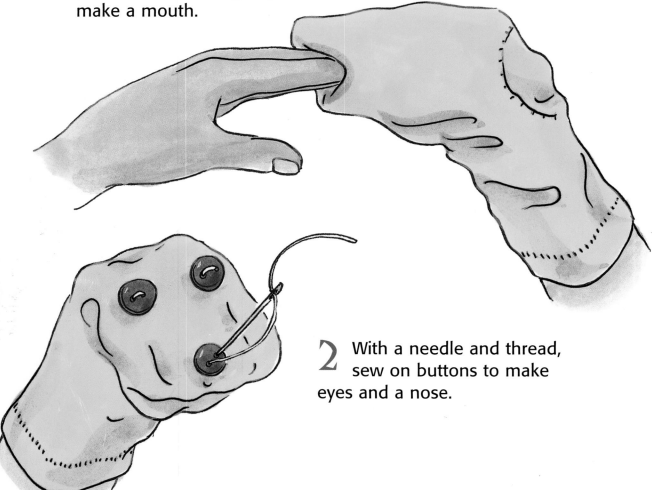

2 With a needle and thread, sew on buttons to make eyes and a nose.

3 To make hair, wind some yarn around a piece of cardboard. Tie a piece of yarn or thread around the loops at one end.

4 Cut across the bottom of the yarn loops with a scissors. Sew the yarn onto the sock using the two tying threads.

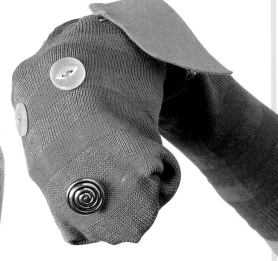

★ Bright Idea ★
Use scraps of felt to add extra
details, such as ears, lips,
or a tongue.

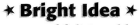

33

Wind Wizard

All it takes is a gentle breath of air to start this whirligig twirling!

You Will Need

- scissors
- egg carton
- paint
- paintbrush
- ice cream sticks
- glue
- metal skewer
- large bead
- ball-headed pin
- modeling clay

1 Cut five cups off of an egg carton. Trim down four of the cups to make them more shallow. Paint all of the cups.

2 Paint two ice cream sticks. When they are dry, glue them together, crossing each other in the middle.

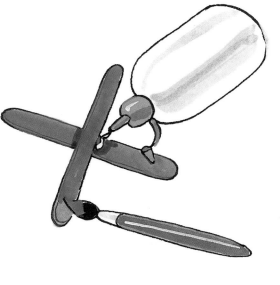

3 Glue a shallow cup onto the end of each stick (as shown). Make sure all of the cups face the same direction.

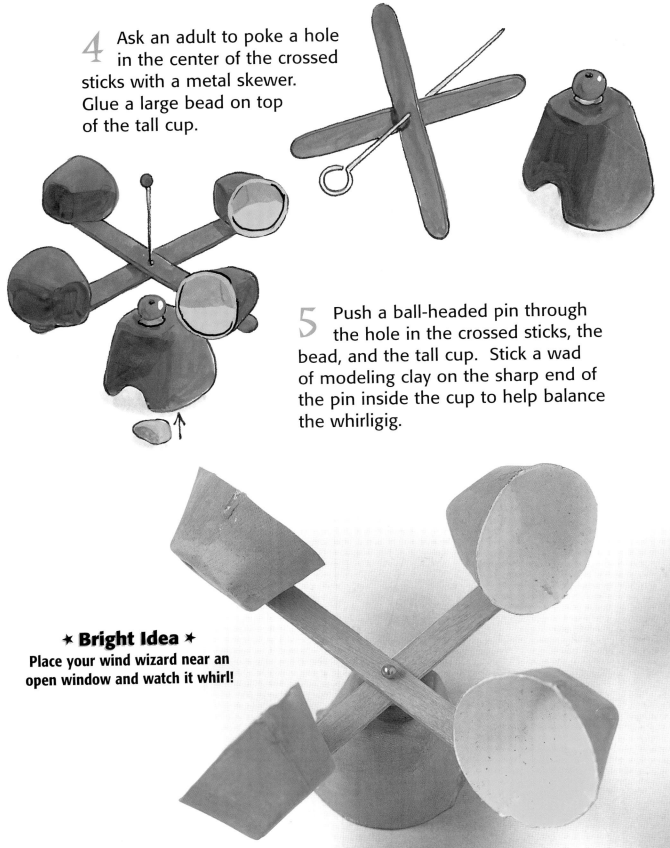

4 Ask an adult to poke a hole in the center of the crossed sticks with a metal skewer. Glue a large bead on top of the tall cup.

5 Push a ball-headed pin through the hole in the crossed sticks, the bead, and the tall cup. Stick a wad of modeling clay on the sharp end of the pin inside the cup to help balance the whirligig.

★ **Bright Idea** ★
Place your wind wizard near an open window and watch it whirl!

Critter Candles

**These crafty salt-dough cuties
will brighten up any table!**

1 Mix a cup of flour with a
cup of salt in a bowl. Add
a cup of water, a little at a time,
until the mixture is a soft dough.
Knead the dough with your hands
until it is smooth.

2 Ask an adult to turn on the oven
to 250° Fahrenheit (120° Celsius).
Roll a spoonful of dough into a ball to
make the body. Roll a smaller ball for
the head. Shape pieces of dough to
make feet, arms, and ears. Press all
of the pieces of dough in place.

3 Push the end of a candle into the dough and wiggle it around so it fits loosely. Remove the candle and place the dough shape in a baking pan.

4 Bake the dough shapes for three hours. Then let them cool completely.

5 Paint the shapes with acrylic paints, then coat them with clear varnish.

★ **Helpful Hint** ★
To make large pieces of dough, such as a rabbit's ears, bake the shapes separately and glue them on afterward.

37

Pop-Up Polly

Surprise your friends with this perky puppet-in-a-pot.

You Will Need
- clean plastic bottle
- craft knife
- scissors
- crepe paper
- rubber band
- thread
- glue
- wooden spoon
- wiggly eyes or marker

1. Ask an adult to cut off the top of a plastic bottle by making a slit in the side of the bottle with a craft knife, then using scissors to cut all the way around.

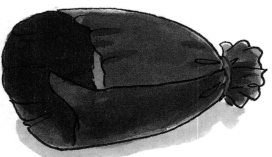

2. Wrap a sheet of crepe paper around the bottle and put a rubber band around it at the neck. Tuck the loose crepe paper at the bottom into the bottle.

3. Cut a narrow strip off of the end of a roll of crepe paper. Tie a piece of thread tightly around the paper loops. Cut across the loops on the opposite side to make a wig.

4 Glue the wig onto the end of a wooden spoon. Glue on some wiggly eyes or draw on eyes with a marker.

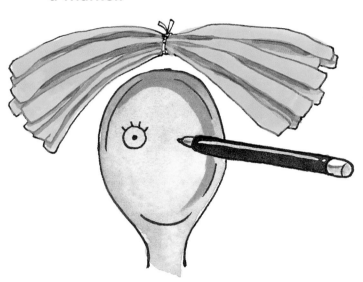

5 Slide the spoon into the bottle so the handle sticks out of the neck. Cover the rubber band around the neck with a crepe-paper bow.

★ **Helpful Hint** ★
Put a rubber band around the end of the spoon handle to help keep Polly in place.

39

Animal Ark

March your animals, two by two, into this shoe-box ship!

1 Snip the corners of a shoe box lid and fold in the sides to make the lid small enough to fit inside the shoe box.

You Will Need
- scissors
- shoe box and lid
- 2 smaller boxes
- paints
- paintbrush
- glue
- corrugated cardboard
- black marker
- pictures of animal faces

2 Place a smaller box, such as a tissue box, inside the shoe box. Fit the lid section over the smaller box to make a deck.

3 Paint the bottom of the ark. Then paint another small box with a different color. Glue the small box onto the ark's deck.

40

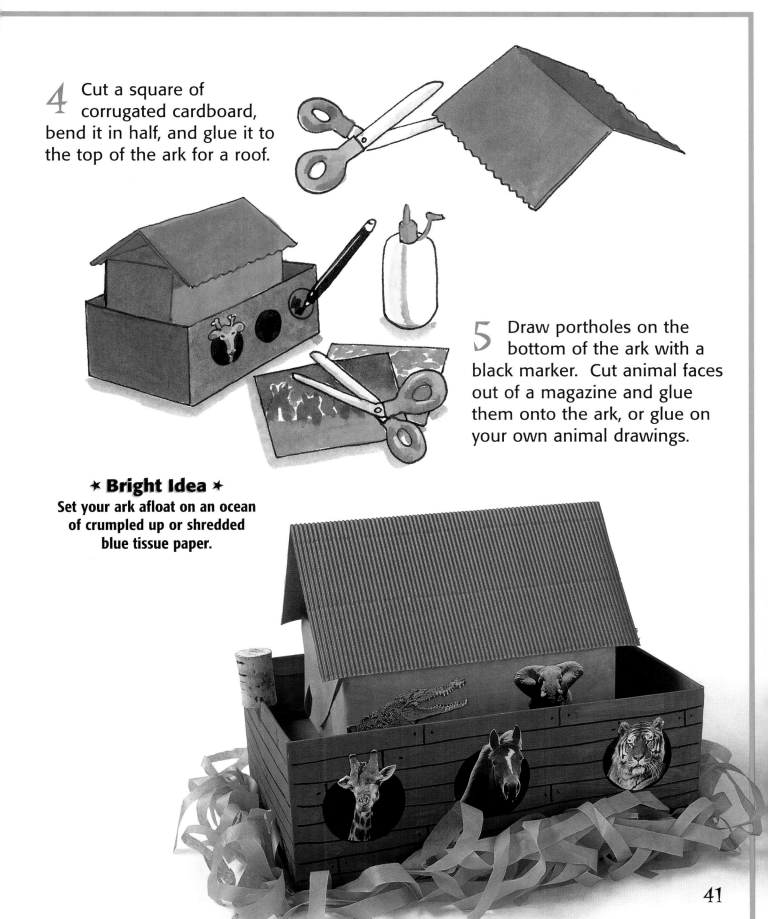

4 Cut a square of corrugated cardboard, bend it in half, and glue it to the top of the ark for a roof.

5 Draw portholes on the bottom of the ark with a black marker. Cut animal faces out of a magazine and glue them onto the ark, or glue on your own animal drawings.

★ **Bright Idea** ★
Set your ark afloat on an ocean of crumpled up or shredded blue tissue paper.

Weather Wheel

Spin this weather wheel to get a report for the day!

1 Set a compass to 4 ½ inches (11 cm) and draw a circle on a piece of cardboard. Reset the compass to 1 ½ inches (4 cm) and draw another separate circle. Cut out both circles.

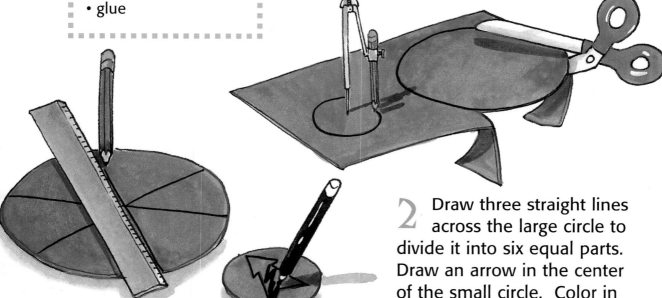

2 Draw three straight lines across the large circle to divide it into six equal parts. Draw an arrow in the center of the small circle. Color in the arrow with a black marker.

3 Poke the compass point through the center of both circles. Push a paper fastener through the hole to hold the circles together. The circle with the arrow should turn easily.

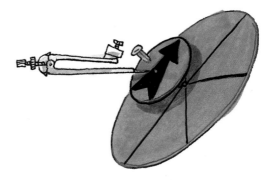

4 Tape a loop of thread or string onto the back of the large circle to hang the weather wheel. Plan your designs for the wheel so this loop is at the top.

5 Cut six designs out of colored cardboard to show different kinds of weather. Glue one design onto each section of the wheel.

★ **Helpful Hint** ★
Draw pictures that show the right kinds of weather for your local area.

Totem Pole

The animal figures on a totem pole have special meanings for the American Indians who carve and paint them. How will your totem pole have special meanings for you?

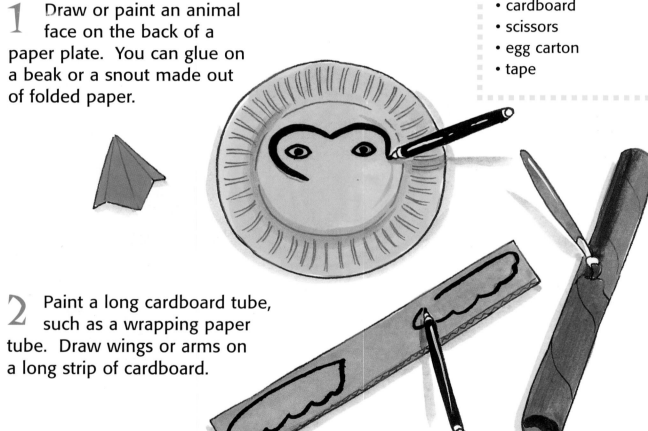

1 Draw or paint an animal face on the back of a paper plate. You can glue on a beak or a snout made out of folded paper.

2 Paint a long cardboard tube, such as a wrapping paper tube. Draw wings or arms on a long strip of cardboard.

3 Cut the lid off of an egg carton. Cut out and paint pairs of egg cups to make animal faces.

You Will Need
- markers
- paints
- paintbrush
- paper plate
- glue
- paper
- long cardboard tube
- cardboard
- scissors
- egg carton
- tape

44

4 Draw or paint a pair of feet on the lid of the egg carton. Cut a hole in the lid and push the cardboard tube into the hole.

5 Tape the paper plate to the top of the pole. Attach the wings, animal faces, and any other figures along the pole beneath it.

★ **Bright Idea** ★
Stand your totem pole outside your bedroom door to mark this room as your special place.

45

Diorama Drama

Build a thrilling undersea scene, a magical moonscape, or a special spot you've seen in your dreams!

1 Cut open both corners on one long side of a shoe box to make a flap.

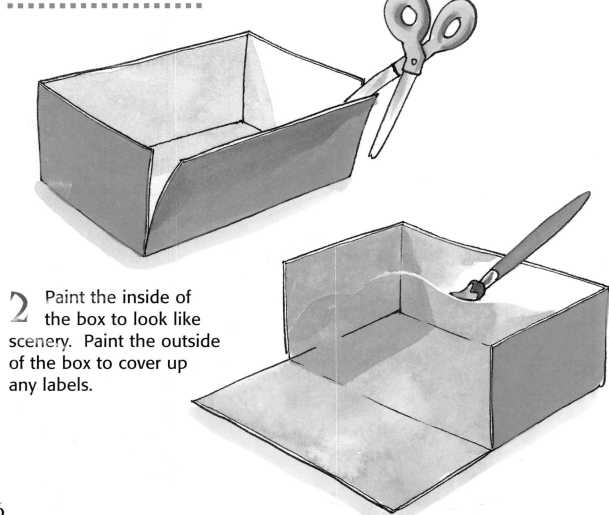

2 Paint the inside of the box to look like scenery. Paint the outside of the box to cover up any labels.

46

3 Make trees and bushes by crumpling colored paper. Use aluminum foil to make a pond and beads to make flowers. Glue all of these pieces in place.

4 Shape modeling clay to make tree trunks and figures to place in your diorama.

★ Helpful Hint ★
To store the diorama, fold up the front flap and put the lid on the box.

Glossary

bias tape: a narrow strip of folded fabric used in sewing to neatly finish seams and hems.

corrugated: having a wrinkled surface or a surface of ridges and grooves.

diorama: a lifelike model scene, usually with a painted background and miniature figures.

knead: to press and squeeze with the hands, over and over.

overlap: to lie over the top of something, partly covering it.

papier-mâché: material made from shredded newspaper, water, and glue that can be molded when wet to form hard, strong, lightweight shapes when it dries.

protractor: a tool with a semicircular shape, used for measuring and drawing angles.

skewer: a pointed stick made of wood or metal, which is used to hold meat together while the meat is roasting.

Styrofoam: the trademark name for a lightweight, foamlike plastic.

swivel: to turn easily on some kind of pivot, or post.

varnish: a sticky, paintlike substance spread over a surface to give it a hard finish and a shiny appearance.

whirligig: a toy that continuously turns or spins when air pushes against it.

More Craft Books by Gareth Stevens

Animal Crafts. Worldwide Crafts (series).
Iain MacLeod-Brudenell

Crafty Masks. Crafty Kids (series).
Thomasina Smith

Crafty Puppets. Crafty Kids (series).
Thomasina Smith

Great Gifts. Handy Crafts (series).
Gillian Souter

Index